how does your
garden grow?

how does your garden grow?

great gardening for
green-fingered kids

Clare Matthews

Photographs by **Clive Nichols**

hamlyn

For my grandmother, Lucy Rudd

First published in Great Britain in 2005 by
Hamlyn, a division of Octopus Publishing Group Ltd
2–4 Heron Quays, London E14 4JP

Copyright © Octopus Publishing Group Ltd 2005
All photographs © Clive Nichols 2005, apart from page 80 (top)
and page 82 (bottom) © Peter Haynes, 2005

Distributed in the United States and Canada by
Sterling Publishing Co., Inc.
387 Park Avenue South, New York, NY 10016-8810

ISBN 0 600 61141 8
EAN 9780600611417

A CIP catalogue record for this book is available from the British Library

Printed and bound in China

10 9 8 7 6 5 4 3 2 1

The author and publisher have made every effort to ensure that all
instructions and ideas given in this book are accurate and safe, but they
cannot accept liability for any injury, damage or loss to either person or
the property whether direct or consequential and howsoever arising.

Measurements
Both imperial and metric measurements have been given throughout
this book. When following instructions, you should choose to work in
either metric or imperial, and never mix the two.

contents

Introduction

This book is packed with simple, achievable projects with masses of child appeal, which can be tackled by young children with help and older children almost unaided. Unashamedly playful, the projects use novelty and ingenuity to capture the children's imagination. Nurturing a pot of plants may have some appeal, but theme that pot so the child is growing her own pasta sauce, attracting butterflies to the garden or growing flowers he can eat – and they are hooked.

By introducing children to the real pleasures and rewards of tending the garden, you will encourage them to consider the minor miracles of nature that abound all around us and initiate them into the thrill of creating an imaginative garden. The colourful pots they tend, the whimsical artworks they create and the treats for wildlife they provide give them a real stake in the garden and something of which they can, quite rightly, be proud. As they explore the world of plants and the garden environment through the projects, I hope that children will be inspired to question the nature of things: Why is grass green? Why do plants have roots? How do plants know when to flower? Many of these searching questions are answered here in simple terms alongside the projects.

CLOCKWISE FROM TOP LEFT *Summer flower and leaf party (see page 126), Flowers for eating (see page 64), Seed harvest (see page 22), Daisy chain pot (see page 16).*

The projects are described in detail, with easy-to-follow step-by-step instructions. They can be faithfully copied, but there is also plenty of scope for children to use their imaginations and make the projects their own by adding their ideas and decorative motifs. None of the projects requires a great deal of space; in fact many of the activities can be easily accommodated on a balcony, and most have been planned with a limited budget in mind.

The projects are divided into four parts: 'Fun with plants' describes methods or reasons to grow plants that are exciting and fun, from creating a wild flower meadow on a window ledge to planting a desert in a pot, while 'Growing food' details many ideas for growing fruit and vegetables in ways that are a little out of the ordinary. 'Wildlife in the garden' is about providing for the needs of wildlife and so enticing them into the garden, and finally 'Things to make and do' encourages children to use their natural creativity to produce art and artefacts to decorate the garden.

Above all else, this book is designed to be fun and to provide a valuable resource of ideas for parents who want to tempt their children into the garden by providing them with entertaining and enlightening things to do.

CLOCKWISE FROM TOP LEFT *Vegetable tunnel (see page 68), Colourful cane tops (see page 98), Psychedelic mobile (see page 132), Apple tree heart (see page 44).*

fun with plants

Nurturing a plant from a tiny seedling to a magnificent flowering specimen has its rewards, but how much more inspiring if your planting has an exciting purpose, a special theme or is part of an experiment into the astounding capabilities of plants.

This section contains projects in which growing plants in a fun way is part of a larger, inspiring objective. Here, children can make a mini desert bloom, discover different scents through a bed of smells, test the determination of bulbs to grow, watch close up the process of germination and discover many more marvels of nature. Giving lustre to the business of gardening, this approach captures the imagination of children and prompts them to explore willingly the wonders of the plant world.

window ledge meadow

Undemanding and easy to grow, wild flowers have an appealing simplicity and cheeriness that will brighten up any window ledge. The small trough – 50 cm (20 in) long and 20 cm (8 in) wide before it starts growing – will produce an abundance of flowers that are particularly attractive to insects. You could keep the turf trough trimmed, but allowing some of the grass to grow up alongside the flowers would complete the meadow effect.

Materials

Sheet of galvanized mesh 90 x 60 cm (3 x 2 ft)
2 rolls of turf
Multi-purpose compost
Packet of wild flower seeds

Tip

Most seed companies do packets of mixed wild flower seeds – some are even specially selected with young gardeners in mind.

1 First form the sides of the trough: fold up 20 cm (8 in) of the mesh on the two long sides of the sheet. You might want to wear gardening gloves to protect your fingers.

2 Cut out a piece from both ends of each vertical side, 20 cm (8 in) horizontally and 18 cm (7 in) vertically. This will give you a tongue of mesh that can be folded up to form the end of the trough, with extra on either side. Fold these flaps round against the long sides of the trough to form the corners.

How do plants grow from tiny seeds?

Inside its hard shell the seed holds the embryo of a new plant. The embryo has all the basic building blocks from which a new plant will grow, but to begin its growth, a process called germination, the seed needs the right conditions of light, warmth and moisture. Once the process begins, the food stored in the seed fuels the embryo as it starts to grow.

4 Roll out a length of turf and cut out a single piece to fit the base, one side and both ends of the trough. Cut a separate piece to fit the remaining long side.

3 Use short lengths of garden wire to fix the corner flaps neatly in position and make the trough sturdy and straight-sided.

5 Carefully line the trough with the turf (grass side out), easing it right into the corners and ensuring that the two pieces butt together well, so there are no gaps. Trim off any overlapping turf.

6 Fill the trough with compost and sow the seeds as directed on the packet. Gently water the compost and keep it slightly moist. Wild flowers thrive in difficult conditions and poor soils, so there is no need to feed or pamper them.

daisy chain pot

Making daisy chains is a simple pleasure that still charms children today, and growing colourful daisies in a pot you have decorated yourself adds to the fun. This pretty pot has been planted with a bright variety of double daisy, *Bellis perennis*, which will provide plenty of flower heads for making daisy chains all summer long. Created with just a few brushstrokes, the painted decoration is easily replicated even by very young children.

Materials

Terracotta pot (it doesn't need to be very large)
PVA glue
Blue, pink, yellow and green acrylic paints
Multi-purpose compost
4 Bellis perennis *plants*

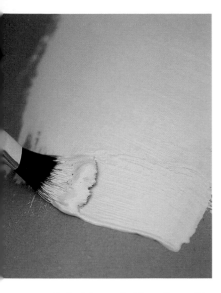

Why do flowers open in the sun and close when it is dark?

This is not strictly true. Although some flowers open and close in response to weather conditions, others respond to the length of the day or open at fixed times. They time their opening to let butterflies, bees or other pollinators reach their pollen. Some flowers even open at night, as they are normally pollinated by bats or moths. In 1751, Carl Linnaeus published his idea for a flower clock with which the time of day could be told (approximately) by which flowers were open.

1 Seal the pot inside and out with a solution of equal parts PVA glue and water. When this is dry, apply a coat of the blue paint. Allow this to dry and, if necessary, apply another coat.

2 When the base coat is completely dry, add the daisies. First, using a single brushstroke, paint four pink petals in a cross shape, then add a petal in each gap to give a total of eight petals for each flower. Add a single dot of yellow paint to give each daisy a golden centre.

3 Paint chains of daisies curling around the pot and join them up with a single brushstroke of green paint.

4 When the paint is completely dry, fill the pot with compost, plant the daisies and water in. Once established, these few plants will produce a regular crop of daisies to make fantastic daisy chains.

growing smells

Children love smells, so choosing and learning about plants by their scented flowers or aromatic leaves is an appealing theme for them to explore. A small fragrant plot to call their own is a great way to stimulate children's interest in plants – not only will their patch be brimming with dazzling blooms to show off, but it will also smell gorgeous.

Materials

7 pegs 20 cm (8 in) long made from 5 x 2.5 cm
(2 x 1 in) wood
String
Log rolls 15 cm (6 in) high and 4 m (13 ft) in total
Wood stain
Garden wire
Loam-based compost

Plants for spring smells

10 dianthus plants
7 lemon thyme plants
5 pots of hyacinths (we used 'Blue Jacket')

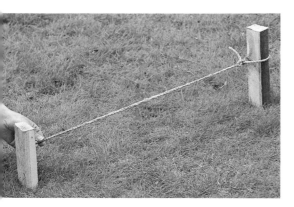

1 Drive a peg into the centre of the area you would like the bed to occupy. Loop a piece of string around the peg so that it extends to a length of 65 cm (26 in). Pull the string taut and drive in a peg at its end.

2 Repeat this process with the remaining five pegs, spacing them equally around the central peg to form a circle. When all the pegs are in position, remove the central peg.

3 Give the log rolls two coats of wood stain and, when they are dry, stretch them around the pegs to form a circle. Using loops of garden wire, attach the roll to the pegs and join the lengths of log roll together. Fill the bed with compost to make it ready for planting.

4 With the plants still in their pots, arrange them on the surface of the compost. Remember to allow space for the plants to grow.

5 When you are happy with the arrangement, remove the plants from their pots and plant them out in the compost bed.

6 Water the plants well. The raised bed will not need much maintenance, just keep the compost moist and remove any dead flowers to encourage more, and on warm spring days the plants in the bed will fill the garden with perfume.

Plants for summer smells

3 chocolate cosmos plants
(Cosmos atrosanguineus)
3 scented day lilies that don't grow
too large (we used Hemerocallis
'Lemon Sorbet')
4 pots of lilies

For a fragrant summer display, the blues and pinks of the spring bed are replaced with warmer shades of orange and yellow and just a touch of deep mahogany. Glamorous and richly fragrant, the blooms of lilies and day lilies (*Hemerocallis*) combine with the smaller round flowers of the chocolate-scented cosmos to make a display that is a treat for both eyes and nose.

LEFT and BELOW *Lilies are a real garden favourite known for their heady fragrance. Not all lilies produce a good scent, and a scentless lily is as disappointing as a beautiful rose or honeysuckle when it does not have the perfume you hope for. The lily bulbs can be left in the bed and should produce a fragrant display again next year.*

ABOVE *Each of the lemon yellow trumpets may last only a day, but Hemerocallis 'Lemon Sorbet' produces them in great profusion and each one smells wonderful. As it is a perennial, the day lily will die back in the autumn and can be left in the bed to flower next year. There are a great many day lilies to choose from, in colours from cream to pink to gold and deep red, but not all are scented, so choose carefully for this project.*

RIGHT *Flowers do not have to smell flowery: the perfume of these velvety cosmos is a real surprise, as they smell just like chocolate. Cosmos will not withstand a harsh winter and so should be taken out of the bed and placed in a greenhouse for the colder months, or treated as an annual.*

How do plants know when to flower?

Each plant has a special time of year when it will normally bloom. Plants have a mechanism that judges this, not from the length of the days or the hours of sunlight, but rather from the length of the night or the hours of darkness.

seed harvest

Once the summer petals have faded, a profusion of crisp brown seed heads stand brimful with valuable seeds. Setting children the task of collecting this seed and designing their own seed packets is an absorbing and fulfilling way to spend a fine autumn day. Prettily decorated packets of home-grown seeds make perfect gifts for children to give to family members, friends and fellow gardeners.

Materials

Brown paper envelopes, one for each type of seed
Crayons or felt-tip pens
Large tin or airtight container

Tip

Choose a dry day, when the seed heads are brittle and easy to crack open.
If the seed is damp when it is collected, it is unlikely to store well.

How do plants spread their seed?

Plants have developed a number of different ways to distribute their seed. Some rely on the wind to carry their seed away from the parent plant; these seeds normally have fluffy parachutes that can be caught by the wind (such as dandelions). Others, such as poppies, have seed heads like pepper pots, and when the wind blows the seeds are shaken out. Some seeds are spread by birds or animals, so they come packed in edible fruit or covered with tiny hooks that catch in an animal's fur. Exploding seedpods are yet another method – when dried by the sun or disturbed by any movement, the pods burst open, spreading seeds.

1 Start by decorating the envelopes, or rather seed packets. Record the plant's name and the date the seed was collected. You could also include the name of the garden it was collected in and the collector.

2 Add a picture of the plant in flower, and perhaps the seed head; this will be a helpful reminder of how the plant looks when you plant your seed next year. You could use gardening books or magazines to help with inspiration for the illustrations.

3 Select the ripest, driest seed heads and shake the seed directly into the envelope. Remove any stray pieces of plant or seed case.

4 Put the sealed envelopes into a large tin or airtight container and store them in a dry place. In the spring, the seeds can be sown in pots or straight into the garden.

growing pips and seeds

A fruit is essentially a tasty seed packet. Normally we eat the flesh and discard the seed, yet saving the seed and coaxing it into life is a terrific opportunity for children to see at first hand the incredible life cycle of plants, from fruit to plant. Even if the climate is not suitable for exotic plants outside, they should grow well inside on a warm window ledge or in a greenhouse.

Good seeds, pips and stones to grow

apple
avocado
date
lemon
mango
orange
papaya
passion fruit
See also *Roots and shoots, page 42, to see how to grow your own oak tree*

Growing an avocado plant

1 Carefully cut the avocado in half and remove the stone. Soak the stone in warm water for 30 minutes.

2 Cut about 1 cm (⅜ in) from the pointed end of the stone and plant it in some compost in a small pot so the cut face of the stone is left exposed. Water it and place it in a warm, light spot.

3 Keep the compost moist and after several weeks the stone will split and a tiny shoot will emerge (don't worry if the stone begins to look mouldy). The seed leaves will then unfurl at the top of the shoot.

4 After a few more days, the shoot will grow taller and, eventually, the first pair of true leaves will appear.

Growing oranges and lemons

1 Cut the orange or lemon in half and remove the pips.

2 Soak the pips in water overnight. Plant them in a small pot of compost to a depth of about 4 cm (1½ in).

3 Water the compost. For the seeds to germinate they will need frequent watering and a temperature of 25–32°C (77–90°F).

4 Following several years of careful nurturing, your lemon tree could look like this. The pots can be moved outside in the summer months.

Mango

● After you have eaten the mango, scrub away as much of the fibre as possible from the large stone.

● Soak the stone in water for two to three days, then gently remove the outer coat.

● Lay the stone on its side, with the curved side uppermost, in a small pot of compost and cover it with a little more compost.

● Place the pot in the airing cupboard or a similar warm place until the seed germinates, then keep the plant in a very warm, sunny spot.

Passion fruit

● Choose a ripe fruit and scoop out some of the seeds and pulp.

● Leave the seeds to ferment for two or three days. This means leaving them, with the pulp still clinging to them, in a little water and placing them somewhere warm. The seed mix will go mouldy, but don't worry – this is part of the process.

● Wash the seeds in a fine sieve. They are now ready to be planted out individually in small pots of seed compost.

● Keep the compost moist. The seeds will need a temperature of at least 20°C (75°F) to germinate, so keep the pot in a warm spot, such as the airing cupboard. Check regularly to see that the compost is not too dry.

● Once the first sign of growth appears, move the pot to a light but still warm place, such as a sunny window ledge – and just watch your passion fruit plants grow. They are climbers, like grapevines, so will need a stick for their tendrils to cling to as they shoot upwards.

tropical island sand pit

Sand pits are great fun for young children but usually add nothing to the look of the garden. But with a majestic banana plant and a little imagination, this everyday play area can evoke a tropical paradise. Its pebbly island has objects to explore and perhaps treasure to find – what this 'tactile pit' contains can be guided by the ages of the children and can be changed periodically to reveal new surprises.

Materials

4 new oak sleepers, each 1.8 m (6 ft) long
Piece of 5 x 10 cm (2 x 4 in) timber about
   80–100 cm (3 ft) long
Large-headed tacks
4 m² (4 sq yd) of thick polythene sheet
Bag of tree and shrub compost
Banana plant (Musa basjoo)
1 m² (1 sq yd) of weed-suppressing membrane
5 bags of play sand
Pebbles, shells and treasure

⚠️ *Note: If cats and other animals are frequent visitors to the garden, provide a lid of marine ply or secure a piece of netting across the top to keep them out.*

1 Arrange the four sleepers in place to form a square, fitting them as closely together as possible. Use sandpaper to remove any sharp edges or splinters.

2 Cut the ends of the piece of timber at 45 degree angles, so that it fits neatly across one corner of the sand pit. Line the larger portion of the pit with polythene, so that about 10–15 cm (4–6 in) of the polythene lap up the side of the sleepers. Puncture a few holes in the polythene for drainage and fix it to the sleepers with large-headed tacks.

Why aren't all leaves the same?

Each leaf type has evolved to help plants adapt to different growing conditions. Plants in shady locations, like the understorey of a rainforest, might have large leaves to help collect more sunlight. Many plants from dry, sunny places, however, have small, grey, downy leaves because gathering sunlight is no problem but losing water is. So having the right type of leaf is all part of a plant's strategy for survival.

3 Fill the smaller section of the pit about two-thirds full with compost and plant your banana plant, watering it well. Cover the surface of the compost with weed-suppressing membrane, tucking in the edges. Cover the membrane with a thick layer of pebbles, shells and treasure.

4 Tip the play sand into the remaining area spreading it out evenly, and the tropical island is ready to be inhabited.

Tropical plant care

Protect the banana plant from frost by either removing its leaves in autumn and wrapping it in a layer of straw, or growing it in a container that can be sunk into the 'island' and moved under shelter for the colder months.

relaxing bath pot

The soothing, relaxing properties of lavender and chamomile are well known. Growing them together in a pot allows children to pick fragrant little posies to perfume their bath and perhaps help them to sleep soundly. Given a warm, sunny spot, both are undemanding plants, easily cared for by children, who will enjoy the pungent fragrance of the lavender and the surprising smell of sweets produced by the chamomile.

Materials

Suitably sized pot
Pebbles or crocks for drainage (old
*   broken flower pots or household*
*   crockery are ideal)*
Multi-purpose compost
Dwarf lavender plant
3 chamomile plants

1 Put a layer of crocks or pebbles in the bottom of the pot to ensure good drainage. Half fill the container with compost, remove the lavender from its pot and place it at the back of the container. Remove the chamomile plants from their pots and arrange them around the front edge of the container.

2 Carefully pack compost around the roots of the plants, firming it in gently so that the level of the compost is the same as it was in the pots.

3 Water the pot well and place it in a sunny spot. Keep the compost just moist but not too damp and the plants should thrive.

The harvest

1 When the lavender and chamomile are in flower, children can pick a small posy to fragrance their bath, making bathtime special. Children's scissors should easily cut through the stems.

2 Tie the tiny posy with a ribbon and hang it in the flow of the warm water. The flowers should release their soothing fragrance into the bathroom.

3 Alternatively, you can simply drop the pretty posy of dried flowers into the bath to float in the water, releasing its perfume as you bathe.

Preserving the scent of summer

Drying the flowers preserves some of the fragrance of summer for winter bathtimes. Cut lavender and chamomile flowers with reasonably long stalks, tie them together and hang them in a warm, dry place. The dried heads will make a lovely pot pourri (see page 134) or they can be used to fill muslin bags or pouches with summer scent.

1 Remove some of the flower heads and place them in the centre of a square of muslin. Only a few flower heads are needed in each pouch.

2 Gather the edges of the muslin together and tie a colourful satin or velvet ribbon around the parcel of flowers. Stored in an air-tight jar, the little pouches will keep their magical scent until the next crop of lavender is ready. The fragrant bundles also make great gifts for children to give, that they have grown and made themselves.

celebration tree

Whether it is the birth of a new baby in the family, starting school or moving into a new house, planting a tree is a great way to mark the occasion. Giving the planting some ceremonial trappings will add to the fun and make it feel special. Not only is a tree a long-lived symbol of a significant event or rite of passage, but also watching how the tree grows is a way of giving the abstract passing of time a physical reality for children.

When to plant?

Trees grown in containers are available at any time of the year, but late autumn is a particularly good time for planting. The soil is still warm from the summer, but trees have slowed down their growth and will transplant well. Through the autumn and winter is also the time when bare-rooted or root-balled trees become available; these are often much better value than container-grown trees, and as long as you can plant them straight away, their roots will get off to a better start.

⚠️ *Note: It is important to choose a tree to suit your garden; it would be upsetting to have to fell a special tree that has grown too large. There are plenty of trees to choose from for even the smallest of gardens.*

1 Choose your site (bearing in mind the final size of the tree) and dig a hole. It should be about twice as wide as the root ball and deep enough so that when the tree is placed in the hole, the soil mark on the trunk is level with the surrounding soil surface. Fork some organic matter into the base of the hole.

2 Lower the tree into the hole, checking the position of the soil mark. Some root-balled trees have special wrappings that can be left on; others will need removing once the tree is in position. If you are using a bare-rooted tree, spread the roots out evenly on a slight dome in the base of the hole.

3 Gradually refill the hole with soil and extra organic matter, stopping every so often to firm the soil and ensuring that the tree is held firmly. Finally, drive a stake into the ground at 45 degrees to the trunk of the tree away from the root ball, and secure the stake to the tree using an adjustable tree tie.

4 Adding a plaque displaying the name of the planter, perhaps together with the date and what the tree planting commemorates, is an important part of the planting.

desert in a bowl

The parched landscape of the desert fascinates and intrigues children. By creating their own potted desert they can grow a range of unfamiliar plants and discover how plants survive in such challenging conditions. A desert garden is easy to care for, and should thrive, even for the most negligent of young gardeners, as long as it occupies a warm, sunny spot and is taken into a heated greenhouse or porch when the weather turns cold.

Materials

Large terracotta bowl-shaped pot
PVA glue
Yellow acrylic paint and sand
Pebbles or crocks for drainage
Multi-purpose compost
Grit
Succulents or cacti
3 rocks
Pebble mulch or coloured aquatic gravel

⚠ *Note: Most good garden centres will boast an array of small cacti and succulents for children to choose from. You can include some spiky cacti, but this version (right) contains only succulents with no significant spikes, which would be safe even for young children.*

1 First make the desert pot. Mix yellow acrylic paint with some PVA glue and a handful of sand and use the mixture to paint the outside of the pot and about the top 10 cm (4 in) down from the rim on the inside. Leave it to dry.

2 Put a good layer of crocks or pebbles in the bottom of the pot (most succulents do not require a great depth of soil to grow in: 15 cm (6 in) is usually sufficient). Fill the pot with a mix of 1 part grit to 3 parts compost to within 5 cm (2 in) of the rim of the pot. With the plants still in their pots, arrange them and the large rocks on the surface of the compost. When you are happy with the desert landscape you have created, plant the succulents or cacti, ensuring the compost around them is at the same level as it was in their pots.

3 Complete the desert with a mulch of natural or coloured pebbles and place it in a sunny position. Water the desert only when the compost is just dry – although these plants will survive long periods of drought, they will grow better with a little moisture in the soil.

ABOVE *The striking flowers produced by some cacti make them a natural centrepiece. The smallest cacti are just 5 cm (2 in) tall, and there is a wide range to choose from.*

ABOVE RIGHT *Never try to hold a cactus – however gentle their spines may appear – they can break off in the skin and cause irritation. Instead, fold a piece of paper into a long strip and hold it firmly around the cactus. You can then safely remove the plant from its pot and place it in its new home. Once the cactus is safely planted, the paper can be removed.*

RIGHT *This version of the desert garden contains spiny cacti and is suitable only for older children to plant out who will not be tempted to handle the cacti. Use the method described above to plant the spiny cacti.*

How do plants survive without water?

All plants need some water, but desert plants have developed ways that allow them to survive without much water and for long periods of time between rainfalls (in some areas it rains only every few years). Succulents store water in fleshy leaves with a waxy coating to reduce water loss. Other plants, such as cacti, have reduced their surface area by dispensing with leaves altogether, so they lose less water by evaporation and store water in an enlarged stem instead.

ABOVE *Plants have evolved into some remarkable and unlikely forms in order to survive in desert and semi-desert regions.*

ABOVE RIGHT *This succulent has vibrant orange flowers and a fluffy, insulating coating on its leaves and flower stems to keep the leaf cool; this is all part of this plant's strategy to survive extreme temperatures.*

upside-down bulbs

Most bulbs are astonishingly easy to grow and reliably produce impressive blooms. This is an experiment to show just how determined they are to grow, whatever the circumstances. We used the sunny yellow tulip 'Monte Carlo', but you could test the mettle of any bulbs you have to hand. Most bulbs should be planted in the autumn and will flower the following spring.

Materials

3 quite deep, narrow, frost-proof pots
9 bulbs
Pebbles or crocks for drainage
Multi-purpose compost
3 labels

What is a bulb?

A bulb is a cluster of very short swollen leaves grouped around a bud. It is the bud that grows and pushes up through the soil to form the plant.

1 Put a layer of broken crocks or pebbles in the bottom of each pot. Add a layer of compost, leaving space above that is a little over twice the height of the bulbs when placed on the compost.

2 Put three bulbs into each pot on top of the layer of compost. Place the first trio the right way up (pointed end uppermost), the next three on their side and the final group upside down.

3 Fill each pot with compost to within 2 cm (¾ in) of the rim, firming it gently. Carefully label which way up the bulbs are in each pot.

4 Water each pot and place them in a very sheltered position in the garden until early spring. They can then be moved into a more prominent spot where the flowers can be enjoyed and the results of the experiment observed.

5 The bulbs planted the right way up have produced a good show of yellow blooms; the bulbs planted on their sides are flowering but not as magnificently as the first pot and; amazingly, the bulbs that were planted upside down have made it, displaying a small show of foliage just as the others are looking their best.

roots and shoots

This simple project for the autumn allows children to observe closely, in all its miraculous detail, exactly how a mighty oak tree starts its life. Germinating the acorn in water will produce a healthy plant as long as it is transplanted into a pot of compost once it has two or three leaves. The success rate for germinating acorns in this way is excellent, with few acorns failing to grow.

Materials

Acorns
Beads
Small glass bowls
Small terracotta pots
Multi-purpose compost

1 Place a layer of beads about 2–3 cm (1 in) deep in the bottom of each glass bowl. In each bowl, sit three acorns on their sides on the surface of the beads and add enough water just to reach the bottom of the acorns.

2 Place the pots on a bright window ledge and keep the water levels topped up. In a surprisingly short time the acorns will begin to grow.

3 First, the shell of the acorn will split and a thick root will appear, which will start to grow down into the water.

Caring for your acorns

4 Next, a delicate shoot appears. Unbelievably, given time, this fragile shoot will become the trunk of a vast oak tree.

5 The first, almost translucent, leaf appears, followed by others.

6 When each tiny oak has two or three leaves, carefully remove it from the beads, trying not to damage the roots, and transplant it into a small terracotta pot filled with compost.

To keep the plants growing strongly, keep them inside until the spring and then gradually allow them to acclimatize to growing outside by placing them outdoors in good weather. Soon they will be able to remain outdoors and will need moving to larger pots.

apple tree heart

Decorative and quirky, this pair of trained fruit trees allows children to grow their own apples even in the smallest of gardens, or even on a balcony. Training the trees to form a heart shape adds to the excitement, and if taken care of they should fruit well for several years. This is a project to have fun with in autumn and winter, when bare-rooted trees are readily available (see page 34).

Materials

Large, frost-proof terracotta pot
Pebbles or crocks for drainage
Loam-based compost
2 one-year-old unstopped apple trees (see below)
Cane or decorative pole
Length of raffia

Tip

The type of rootstock on to which a fruit tree is grafted regulates its size: pot-grown trees need to be on a dwarfing rootstock. You also need young trees that are still just a single stem. Ask for whips, which are just a year old and have not been pruned (stopped). Choose from the many self-pollinating varieties of apple, which do not depend on other apple trees for pollination.

1 Put a good layer of crocks or pebbles into the bottom of the pot to ensure good drainage. Cover the crocks or pebbles with a generous layer of compost, firming it well.

2 Push the cane or pole into the centre of the pot. Place the fruit trees in position so that they are sloping away from each other, spreading their roots out evenly. Add more compost to within 5 cm (2 in) of the rim. Before firming, adjust the position of the trees so that the soil mark on the trunk is level with the surface of the compost in the pot.

3 Ensure that the soil level is at least 10 cm (4 in) below the level of the graft scar on the lower part of the stem. If the graft is covered with soil, the tree may send out roots from above the graft and the dwarfing effect of the rootstock will be lost.

4 Carefully bend the trees in towards the cane to form a heart shape and fasten them to the cane with a raffia bow. When you are happy with the shape, firm the compost around the trees and water them well. Place your tree in a bright spot and keep the compost moist.

Pruning

To develop and maintain the heart shape, your tree will need pruning. This is not as daunting as it might sound; errors are not a disaster. You are aiming for a halo of growth close to the main heart shape, so:

● In the first summer, when the bases of the shoots have become woody, prune back the new shoots off the main stems to three leaves. Trim side shoots back to one leaf.

● In the winter, prune back any shoots that are causing congestion or over-crowding.

● In the following summer, prune new growth back to one leaf and any new shoots off the main stem to three leaves. (The pruning plan to follow is described in gardening books for cordon trees.) Always cut the shoots back to a bud, and cut at an angle that slopes away from the bud.

ABOVE *You are unlikely to get fruit from your tree in the year you plant it, but in subsequent years your patience will be rewarded with pretty blossom to enjoy in the spring and a crop of juicy apples in the autumn.*

fun with plants **47**

growing
food

Growing real food gives children great satisfaction. When you have nurtured a plant from a seedling, or perhaps even a seed, the moment you make that eagerly awaited harvest is a proud one. One bonus of children growing their own fruit and vegetables is that even the fussiest of eaters are unable to resist trying food they have grown themselves.

Growing fruit and vegetables is not difficult and does not have to involve a huge investment of time and energy, or even a great deal of space, to be a success. The projects here range from the quick and easy, yet immensely rewarding, mini salad garden and wild strawberry ball to the larger scale vegetable tunnel, which will require more commitment, but none of the projects is difficult or requires any special horticultural knowledge. To avoid disappointing results and conflict, however, be realistic about how much responsibility your child is likely to take and be prepared to take on the rest.

wild strawberry ball

Scattered over ice cream or eaten straight from the plant, the tiny, intensely flavoured fruits of the wild strawberry are a real treat. These strawberries are natives of open woodland and can produce a profusion of delicious miniature berries with little attention. Growing them in a suspended sphere is a novelty that appeals to children and is a useful space-saving option that guarantees a good harvest where there is little room to spare.

Materials

*2 round-bottomed wire hanging
  baskets, 30 cm (12 in) across*
2 fibre basket liners to fit the baskets
*10 wild strawberry plants
  (Fragaria vesca)*
Multi-purpose compost
Garden wire

1 Remove the chains from the hanging baskets. Setting the baskets in the top of a bucket while you work will make things easier. Put the fibre liners into the baskets and cut five holes in the liner of each basket, one in the bottom and four spaced evenly around the sides.

2 Gently, push the foliage of one of the plants through the hole in the liner at the base of a basket. This is much easier to do if you wrap the foliage in a sleeve of paper.

3 Now add four plants at the sides of the basket in a similar fashion. Gently work some compost around the root balls and then completely fill the basket with compost. Plant up the second basket in the same way.

4 Firm the compost well and water each basket thoroughly to ensure the compost is moist before the ball is assembled. If the compost settles after watering, add more to the basket, as it is important that there are no air gaps once the two halves are joined.

5 Sandwich the two baskets together and join them with lengths of stout garden wire. Attach one set of the chains you removed to the top of the ball and hang it in a sunny or partially-shaded position. Keep the ball moist by watering slowly from the top, and by early summer there should be plenty of tiny strawberries to enjoy.

Why are strawberries red?

Many fruits are brightly coloured to attract the attention of wildlife, such as birds. They eat the fruit and with it the seeds of the plant. As the seeds are indigestible, they pass through the digestive system and are deposited some way from the parent plant. So having attractive fruits is a way for some plants to spread their seeds.

mini salad garden

Harvesting a crop that they have tended themselves is a proud moment for children, and they love eating and sharing the food they have grown. A wooden wine box makes an ideal child-sized vegetable plot.

Decorating the box allows children to personalize their garden, and potato printing is easy enough for even the youngest artist.

Materials

Wooden wine box
Non-toxic acrylic paint in two colours
Potato, cut in half
Black dustbin liner
Pebbles or crocks for drainage
Multi-purpose compost
*Small vegetable plants, such as salad
 leaves and parsley, or seeds*

1 Paint the box with one or two coats of acrylic paint. While it is drying, cut a potato print stamp into the shape of a sun. Children can draw the design on to the cut surface of the potato and leave the cutting out to an adult.

2 Coat the stamp with paint then try a few practice stamps on paper to perfect the technique. Then press the stamp on to the box in an evenly spaced pattern.

3 When the paint is dry, drill a few holes in the base of the box and line it with the black bin liner, piercing a few holes in the bag. Add a layer of small crocks or pebbles to the bottom of the box and fill the lined box with compost to about 2 cm (¾ in) below the rim.

Why do plants have roots?

The roots of a plant do two important things: the thicker roots hold the plant securely in the ground and the little roots take in the water and the goodness from the soil. The water and minerals are transported up the roots and the stem of the plant to the leaves. The stem acts like a straw and is called the xylem.

4 Plant or sow an edging of parsley around colourful 'cut and come again' salad leaves. Children can choose their favourite herbs and leaves and plant or sow them in their own design.

5 Water the box contents well and place it in a sunny spot. Keep the box watered and watch the plants grow.

grow-your-own pasta sauce

The promise of growing a favourite meal in their own garden container is a terrific way to encourage children's gardening talents. Thanks to the many patio and dwarf varieties of fruit and vegetables available, it is possible to grow almost everything you need for a pasta sauce in one large pot. The planted pot will need little attention to thrive, just a warm and sheltered location, watering and a regular feed of tomato food once the plants flower.

Materials

Large terracotta pot
PVA glue and acrylic paint (optional)
Pebbles or crocks for drainage
Multi-purpose compost
Bush cherry tomato plant
Patio pepper plant
Patio aubergine plant
Herb plants: we chose oregano and chives,
*   but basil, parsley and others are all good*
*   with pasta and pizza*
Plant labels

1 Painting the pot a cheerful colour will show off the fresh green of the plants and bright fruits. Start by putting a layer of pebbles or crocks in the base of the pot and then fill the pot with compost to about 10 cm (4 in) from the rim.

2 Plan the arrangement of your plants in the pot. Remember to consider the plants' different habits: the aubergine and pepper will grow tall while the tomato will be happy sprawling chaotically over the rim of the pot.

3 Once you are happy with the arrangement, carefully remove the plants from their pots, make a small hole in the compost and put them in, firming the compost around them.

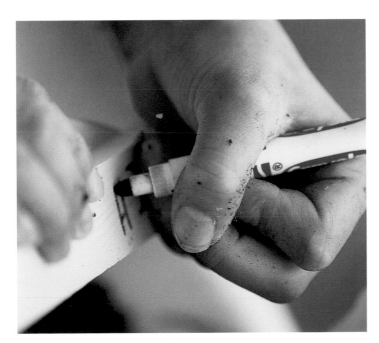

4 Chunky plant labels look decorative and provide plenty of space for children to record the varieties planted. These are made from painted lengths of wood, which can be written on in marker pen (or see Lots of labels, page 122, for other ideas).

5 Water the pot well and place it in a very sheltered, sunny position. For a healthy crop, do not allow the compost to dry out and maintain regular feeds throughout the growing season.

Easy pasta sauce

Preparation time: 10 minutes
Cooking time: 15 minutes
Serves: 4

300 g (10 oz) dried penne pasta

3 tablespoons olive oil

1 onion, chopped

1 medium aubergine, diced

1 green pepper, cored, deseeded
   and diced

1 garlic clove, crushed

1 tablespoon chopped basil

325 g/11 oz cherry tomatoes, halved

1 teaspoon caster sugar

3 tablespoons tomato purée

salt and pepper

1   Cook the pasta according to the packet instructions, then drain.
2   Meanwhile, heat the oil in a large saucepan. Add the onion, aubergine
   and pepper and fry gently for 3–4 minutes.
3   Add the garlic, basil, tomatoes and sugar and fry quickly for 1 minute,
   stirring continuously.
4   Add the tomato purée and 6 tablespoons of water, then season to taste
   with salt and pepper. Bring to the boil and simmer for 5 minutes.
5   Toss the pasta through the sauce, garnish with basil and eat immediately.

BELOW *Presiding over the cooking of a meal made from ingredients you have grown yourself is hugely satisfying. Success will stimulate children's interest not only in plants but also in the food they eat.*

RIGHT *The reward for a few months of care and attention: the home-grown meal-from-a-pot is an occasion to share with family and friends.*

hanging vegetable garden

Hanging baskets do not have to be restricted to colourful annuals. A collection like this makes an unusual, space-saving vegetable gardens, and the range of mini vegetable seeds available means that children can choose and grow their own favourites. Each basket contains plants grown in a different way: one sown with seed, one with plants grown from seed started at home and one from small plants bought from a garden centre.

Materials

3 hanging baskets
Seeds of miniature vegetables (we have used
*   carrots, parsnips, squashes and peppers, but*
*   there are plenty of others to choose from)*
Nasturtium (Tropaeolum majus) seeds
Perpetual spinach plant
Calendula plant
Multi-purpose compost

Tip

To allow children to tend their own baskets, mount them on lengths of strong twine or purpose-made pulley mechanisms, so they can be lowered for watering and thinning out and then hoisted back up.

Root vegetable basket

This basket contains miniature carrots and parsnips grown from seed planted straight into the basket. A nasturtium adds a splash of colour. This basket can usually be planted from early spring to early summer. You could devote a number of baskets to root crops and sow them at intervals, extending the harvest to early autumn.

1 Young children can find handling small seeds difficult. Open the packets and pour a small portion out so they can be easily pinched up for sprinkling.

2 Ensure the basket liners have drainage holes. Fill the basket with compost, firming it gently.

3 Sow an area of carrots and an area of parsnips, lightly sprinkling the seeds on the surface of the compost and covering them with 1 cm (⅜ in) of compost. Add one or two nasturtium seeds to one side to give colour. Water the basket well using a fine rose head.

4 When the carrots and parsnips are about 2–3 cm (1 in) high, thin them out so the plants are about 4 cm (1½ in) apart. Keep the basket well watered, and the carrots and parsnips should be ready to harvest from midsummer onwards.

Pepper and squash basket

1 Both the peppers and squashes are best started in trays or small pots in a greenhouse or on a warm window ledge. Plant two squash seeds 3 cm (about 1 in) deep in a 10 cm (4 in) pot, and seal each pot into a polythene bag until the seedlings germinate. Grow the squash plants indoors until all risk of frost has passed and then acclimatize them to conditions outside over 7–10 days before planting them into the basket.

2 Sow the peppers in small pots under a fine layer of compost and treat them in the same way as the squashes. When they are ready, move the plants into the hanging basket and hang it with the others. The peppers will require a very warm location to thrive.

Spinach and calendula basket

1 Using small plants from a garden centre is a great short cut if you don't have the time or space to raise plants inside. It also cuts out the uncertainties of germination and means that you can catch up if you start planning your vegetable garden late in the year.

2 Fill the basket with compost and plant one calendula and one perpetual spinach plant. Water them in. The leafy green spinach will provide tender leaves for salads or cooking all through the summer and into the autumn, while the golden calendula petals are great sprinkled on rice or salads or added to sandwiches.

flowers for eating

Eating flowers from the garden is just the kind of thing that fascinates children. Many garden blooms are edible, but a good number are not, so it is important that children learn to eat only what they know is allowed – growing their own edible flowers in a pot is a good way to highlight the difference. Plant this pot up early in the spring ready for eating its flowers in late spring. See the next pages for ideas for summer edibles.

Materials

Pot
Pebbles or crocks for drainage
Multi-purpose compost
4 viola plants
Cowslip (Primula veris) *plant*

Spring flowers

1 Put a layer of crocks or pebbles in the pot for drainage and cover with a thick layer of compost.

2 Remove the violas from their pots and arrange them around the edge of the pot, then place the cowslip at the centre. Add more compost and firm it around the plants. Finally, water the pot well.

3 Keep the compost in the pot moist, and by mid-to late spring there should be a good crop of both flowers.

4 Harvest the cowslip flowers in spring before they fade, and pick the violas regularly to encourage more throughout the summer.

Summer flowers

Two easy-to-grow summer favourites, scented pelargoniums and sunflowers, make a good choice for a summer container of edible flowers. The sunny yellow petals of the sunflower can be sprinkled on to salads or even mashed potatoes and used in sandwiches to add colour and taste. The flowers of the pelargonium can be crystallized and used to decorate desserts and cakes.

ABOVE *The bright blooms of nasturtiums have a savoury peppery taste and appealing colour that makes them a great addition to salads or sandwiches.*

LEFT *Once crystallized, the dainty flowers of scented pelargoniums look great on trifles and cakes.*

FAR LEFT *Sunflower petals are an irresistibly colourful garnish on an open sandwich of cream cheese and herbs.*

Crystallized flowers

Covered in a frosting of sugar, crystallized flowers make spectacular decorations for cakes and desserts. Cowslips, violas, violets, rose petals and scented geraniums all look stunning when crystallized. The process is very straightforward and is the same whichever flower you are using.

Materials

Flowers
Gum arabic
Caster sugar

1 Pick your chosen flowers just before you are ready to use them, choosing only those with petals in perfect condition and recently opened.

2 Dissolve 1 teaspoon of gum arabic in 1½ tablespoons of water on a saucer. Paint the mixture on to both sides of the flowers. The stems and heels of the flowers should be removed, but children sometimes find it easier to hold these while working, so they can be gently removed before the flowers are left to dry.

3 Carefully sprinkle the flowers with caster sugar so they are well coated on both sides. Leave the flowers to dry in a warm place until they become crisp. Once dry, they should keep for up to two months in an airtight container.

4 Apply a small blob of icing to a fairy cake and top with a crisp crystallized viola. The humble fairy cake is now fit for a princess.

vegetable tunnel

Once this crawl-through tunnel is covered in the twining stems of beans and mange-tout it becomes a secret den, a great place to lie and enjoy mange-tout straight from the plant. This tunnel could be constructed along the front of a bed or the side of a lawn. It is 2.7 m (9 ft) long, but you could use more or fewer hoops. Use beans with different-coloured flowers and coax a few trailing nasturtiums over the tunnel for a colourful display.

Materials

Weed-suppressing membrane
Membrane pins
16 garden canes 70 cm (28 in) long
13.6 m (45 ft) of hosepipe
String
16 runner bean plants (varieties used
  here are 'Lady Di', 'Desiree' and
  'Sunset')
14 mange-tout plants

1 Clear an area of ground and dig in some good garden compost. Lay out the weed-suppressing membrane to cover 2.7 m x 75 cm (9 ft x 2½ ft) in the centre of the area and firmly pin it down. Push the canes into the ground about 35–40 cm (14–16 in) along both long sides of the membrane. Ensure that each pair is lined opposite each other, and that they are all vertical and secure.

2 Cut 8 lengths of piping 1.7 m (5 ft 6 in) long and push each piece on to a pair of opposing canes to form an arch. Push the pipe right on to the cane so the ends are pushed into the soil.

3 Tie lengths of string horizontally from one arch to the next, looping it around each arch and securing it with a knot. Five strings, one along the top and two running along each side, should be sufficient. Then the tunnel is ready for planting.

4 Plant a runner bean plant at the foot of each arch of pipe and a mange-tout plant in the alternate spaces between the arches. You could grow the plants from seed on a window ledge or in a greenhouse, or alternatively plant them later in the spring straight into the ground.

growing food **69**

Miniature market garden

If you have the space and enthusiasm you could provide a large plot for children to grow a whole range of crops. The rewards can be considerable, both in the sense of achievement for the children and in providing fresh organic vegetables for family meals. However old and enthusiastic the children are, they will inevitably require some adult help to make the project a success, even if it is only advice and encouragement, or helping out with the heavy work.

FAR LEFT *If children are going to perform real gardening work, they will need appropriately sized tools; adult tools are often too large and heavy for children to use effectively.*

ABOVE *Festooned with flowers, pods and twining stems, it doesn't take long for the tunnel to become a leafy private space. To ensure the tunnel is well covered, you may need to gently encourage the beans along the horizontal strings.*

LEFT *To give the tunnel extra privacy, blocks of calendula and perpetual spinach have been planted along the sides of the tunnel to make a colourful, leafy wall. Calendula is of great value in the vegetable plot as it flowers prolifically and encourages beneficial insects and the orange petals can be eaten in salads.*

ABOVE *Here the tunnel is a centrepiece for a larger vegetable plot. The board edging sets the area apart, while brightly coloured stepping stones, a scarecrow (see page 102) and flashing bird scarer (see page 108) have allowed the children to stamp their personality on the garden. Along with the crops growing over the tunnel, the plot includes magnificent red cabbages, wild strawberries, perpetual spinach, calendula and squashes.*

Why do beans always wind around their support in the same direction?

This is just what beans do: all runner bean plants are pre-programmed to spiral around their support in the same direction wherever they are grown. If you look around you will notice that some types of plant always spiral clockwise, while others always spiral anti-clockwise.

wildlife in the garden

For many young children the only outdoor space they are free to explore alone is the garden. Encouraging wildlife into the garden is a fantastic way to stimulate children's enthusiasm for nature and engender respect for the environment.

Few of us live in a rural setting, and enticing what wildlife we can into our gardens not only provides children with an interesting diversion but also helps often hard-pressed native populations of birds and animals to thrive.

Most of us strive for a neat and tidy garden, so we manicure lawns, banish weeds and grow plants for their beauty rather than their attraction to wildlife. Making some provision for wildlife, however, does not have to compromise the look of the garden. Even the small projects in this section will help to increase the number of native species and provide children with a variety of stimulating craft activities, with the promise of watching birds and insects in their own garden.

butterfly pot

On a warm summer's day the colourful, dancing progress of butterflies as they flit from flower to flower, always just out of reach, is captivating for even the youngest of children. The best way to encourage these beautiful visitors to linger in the garden is to provide a ready source of their favourite, nectar-rich blooms. Packed with the flowers that butterflies love, this potted butterfly garden makes a colourful addition to the patio or balcony.

Materials

Large bowl-shaped terracotta pot
PVA glue
Acrylic paints
Pebbles or crocks for drainage
Loam-based compost
2 Aubrieta plants
Marjoram plant
Golden thyme plant
Scabious plant

1 First decorate the pot. Seal it inside and out with a solution of equal parts PVA and water and leave to dry. Then apply a coat of paint to the exterior of the pot. Apply a second coat if necessary. When the paint is dry, paint colourful butterflies randomly around the pot.

2 When the butterfly design is dry, put some crocks or pebbles in the base of the pot, then fill the pot to within 5 cm (2 in) of the rim with compost.

3 Place the plants in the pot and decide how they should be positioned. When you are happy with the arrangement, remove the plants from their pots and fill in around them with compost. Water the pot well and place it in a sunny spot where you can observe the host of butterflies that will pay a visit.

Why do butterflies visit flowers?

Butterflies depend on flowers for their food. When they sit on a flower, they are using a long tongue, called a proboscis, to drink nectar from the flower. When they are not drinking, the proboscis curls up like a Catherine wheel under their head.

There is a host of other plants that will attract butterflies, so you could choose any of those listed below:

asters • chrysanthemums • primulas • *Sedum spectabile* • thymes • Michaelmas daisies • buddlejas (dwarf varieties) • thrifts • helichrysums • achilleas

a stumpery

Even a small area of managed decay will encourage a greater diversity of insect life into the garden, and children can see at close hand the busy world of insects. Lush with fresh green ferns, this stumpery proves that making provision for wildlife does not have to spoil the look of the garden. As the logs rot they will become home to colonies of minibeasts, while the damp nooks and crannies will provide shelter for frogs and toads.

Materials

6 or 7 logs of different sizes
5 ferns

Choosing plants

Ferns for dry conditions:
Hart's tongue fern (*Asplenium scolopendrium*)
Male fern (*Dryopteris filix-mas*)
Soft shield fern (*Polystichum setiferum*)

Ferns for damp conditions:
Autumn fern (*Dryopteris erythrosora*)
Maidenhair fern (*Adiantum pedatum*)
Japanese painted fern (*Athyrium niponicum* 'Pictum')

1 Choose a shady corner of the garden and excavate a hole about 20 cm (8 in) deep and wide enough to accommodate all your logs when placed on their ends. If you have chosen a very tall log, it may be necessary to make part of the hole deeper.

2 Arrange the logs in the hole standing on their ends; aim for an interesting stepped arrangement. Leave some gaps between the logs to plant ferns. When you are happy with the arrangement, pack soil around the logs to hold them securely in place.

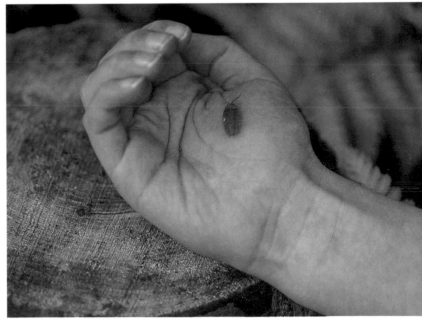

3 Remove the ferns from their containers and plant them around the logs and in the gaps in between. Water the whole stumpery.

4 As the logs begin to decay, many insects or their larvae will move in. Carefully peel away a section of bark (always replacing it afterwards) to observe the thriving world beneath.

sparkling mosaic bird bath

The splashing and flapping of bathing birds is a delight to watch, and access to fresh water is important to birds all year round, not just for bathing but also for drinking and cooling off in hot weather. Transformed with a durable layer of scintillating glass beads, a terracotta plant saucer makes an attractive encouragement for birds to bathe in the garden. Florists' beads give plenty of scope for children to use their creativity.

Materials

Terracotta saucer
Light and dark blue florists' beads
Cement-based tile adhesive
Cement-based tile grout

1 Using a pencil, mark a gently undulating watery design on the terracotta saucer.

2 Mix some tile adhesive and, using a spatula or palette knife, apply a thin layer to a small area of the design, then push the florists' beads into the adhesive, leaving as little gap between them as possible. Continue working, a small area at a time, until the whole of the inside surface of the saucer is covered. Leave the adhesive to dry.

3 Mix some grout as directed by the manufacturer and, using a soft cloth or sponge, wipe it over the beads, pushing the grout into the gaps between them.

4 Remove the excess grout with a clean cloth and polish the surface of the mosaic clean. When the grout is dry, the bird bath is ready for use.

5 Use an upturned pot as a plinth and position the bird bath where the birds can bathe safely away from stalking predators. Keep the bath topped up with fresh water.

funky bird feeder

One of the easiest and most interesting forms of wildlife for children to observe are birds, which are easily coaxed into the garden by a ready supply of food. This contemporary alternative to the traditional bird table allows all types of food to be suspended from its simple structure, broadening the range of birds it will be possible to attract. The tripod is easy to construct, takes up little space and can be set in an area of lawn or planting.

Materials

3 copper pipes 2 m (6 ft) long
Seagrass twine
2 terracotta pots
Terracotta saucer
Seed bell
Peanuts and birdseed

1 Bind a length of twine around all three copper pipes at about their mid point and tie it securely.

2 Splay the pipes out to form a stable tripod shape and place it in its final position, pushing the ends of the pipes into the ground to secure.

3 Tie loops of twine around the neck of the terracotta pots and under the rim of the saucer. Attach long lengths of twine to the loops, so that when suspended by the string the pots hang at an angle. Attach three lengths to the saucer so it will hang level.

4 Attach the pots, saucer, seed bell and strings of peanuts to the copper tripod, in a balanced arrangement, tying them all securely. Finally, fill the pots and saucers with food (see overleaf for examples).

ABOVE AND TOP *Providing a range of foods will attract many species of birds: seed mixes, nuts, chopped apples and some kitchen scraps will all be welcome.*

ABOVE *Instead of using copper, you could spray the metal bars and saucers with silver paint to produce this slick, shiny version.*

peanut ring

Encouraging birds into the garden is a simple task – providing a good source of food, especially at the times of the year when food is scarce, is guaranteed to do the trick. This tempting treat for birds looks good and should attract species such as finches and tits, which will amuse watchers as they manoeuvre, pecking the nuts in their shells.

Materials

Unshelled peanuts
About 1 m (3 ft) of thin- or medium-gauge wire
Raffia

1 Make holes through the shells of the peanuts using a skewer.

2 Bend a length of wire into a circular shape. Form one end into a hook with a straight neck (like a coat hanger). Take care, as the ends can be sharp. Thread the peanuts on to the wire up to the neck, leaving about 10 cm (4 in) empty.

3 Twist the bare end of wire around the hook's neck to close the ring. Tie a raffia bow around the top. The ring is now ready to be hung in a tree or bush, or from a pergola or the Funky bird feeder (see page 82).

pebble ponds

Robust and colourful rubber tub trugs make wonderful child-friendly container ponds, ideal for growing an interesting collection of marginal aquatic plants. Filling the ponds with cobbles or gravel makes them a safer option than a larger pond and they should still prove attractive to aquatic insects. A clutch of brightly coloured ponds makes a striking focal point and will accommodate a variety of plants to provide year-round interest.

Materials

3 tub trugs
2 bags of cobbles or gravel
Aquatic plants
   striped sedge (Carex muskingumensis *'Variegatus')*
   double marsh marigold (Caltha palustris *'Flore Pleno')*
   water mint (Mentha aquatica)
   horsetail (Equisetum hyemale)
   Acorus gramineus *'Ogon'*
   purple loosestrife (Lythrum salicaria)

Tip

If possible, construct the ponds in their final position, since they are very heavy and difficult to manoeuvre once full of pebbles, water and plants.

1 Put a layer of pebbles in the bottom of each trug. All the plants used here will tolerate up to about 15 cm (6 in) of water over their root ball, so the pebbles should come to about 20–30 cm (8–12 in) below the rim of the trug.

2 Arrange the plants in the trugs on top of the layer of pebbles. Once you are happy with their positions, remove their pots.

3 Use a hosepipe or watering can to fill the trug carefully with water to within 20 cm (8 in) of the rim.

4 Gently build up more pebbles around the plants, until the compost around their root balls is completely covered. Add more water so the pebbles are just covered. Keep the water level topped up, especially in hot weather.

ABOVE *In a container of its own, the eye-catching, architectural* Equisetum hyemale *looks impressive and proves that sometimes one dramatic plant can be just as effective as a multitude of smaller ones.*

RIGHT TOP *Unfamiliar and intriguing, the forms of some water plants make them especially appealing to grow.*

RIGHT *The pretty flowers of the double marsh marigold and the variegated leaves of* Acorus gramineus 'Ogon' *combine to make a colourful container display.*

Other aquatic plants

LEFT TOP *Purple loosestrife (Lythrum salicaria) sends up spires of pretty pink flowers in midsummer.*

LEFT *A single pygmy water lily can be grown successfully in a large container and should produce floating blooms through the summer.*

ABOVE *Growing in just 15 cm (6 in) of water Lysichiton camtschatcensis is a vigorous plant that produces a mass of dramatic foliage and striking white spathes.*

compost wormery

Watching worms as they recycle kitchen waste into compost allows children to understand the important role worms play in the health of garden soil. Voracious brandling worms are used in the wormery, as they eat their way more quickly through waste than garden worms. The compost is rich in nutrients – in fact, the worms do such a great job that it is too rich to be used alone and should be mixed with ordinary compost.

Materials

Small plastic or metal bin with a lid
Gravel
Sheet of plastic or bin liner
A few handfuls of potting compost
Kitchen waste (see below)
Torn-up newspaper
Brandling worms

Tip

Striped brandling worms are widely available by mail order and from some garden centres. They will eat most kitchen waste, but do not give them citrus rind, which is too acidic, or meat and bones, which will make the wormery smell.

1 Make several holes in the base of the bin using a hammer and large nail. Next, put a layer of gravel in the base of the bin to create a sump for excess fluid.

2 Puncture the sheet of plastic several times and place it over the stones. This prevents the worms and waste from falling into the sump.

3 Add a layer of potting compost 2–3 cm (1 in) deep on top of the plastic. This provides grit for the worms' digestion.

Looking after your wormery

Keep the wormery in a sheltered spot away from direct sunlight and protected from frosts. Add more waste and newspaper when the worms have got to work on the first layer. Keep this up for about two months and you should be able to sieve out some precious compost. Leave some composted material in the bin as this will contain eggs for the new generation of worms.

4 Add the first batch of kitchen waste to form a layer about 10 cm (4 in) thick and add a small amount of damp shredded newspaper to stop the wormery becoming too compacted.

5 Finally, introduce the worms to their new home, put on the lid and place it on a large pot saucer to catch any liquid that seeps out. Diluted, this liquid makes a great plant food.

a worm observatory

If you could take a cross-section of the soil in your garden, you would see the important work worms do in breaking down organic matter and aerating the soil with their many tunnels. The next best thing is to set up a transparent wormery where you can watch worms at work. Constructing the wormery with a hollow core is important, otherwise the worms would hide in the centre and you wouldn't be able to see them.

Materials

A large transparent container or bottle and a
    slightly smaller container or bottle
Gravel
Multi-purpose compost

Sand
Leaf mould
Grass cuttings
Garden worms

1 Put the small container inside the large one. Put a layer of gravel around the bottom of the outer container.

2 Next, add a layer of compost about 2–3 cm (1 in) deep. Follow this with a layer of sand and then a layer of leaf mould. Keep adding alternate layers until you are within about 4 cm (1½ in) of the top.

3 Sprinkle the top with grass cuttings and decaying leaves and moisten the compost slightly. Now gently put four or five worms on top of the compost. Wrap the wormery in thick black plastic or newspaper and put it in a dark place.

4 After a week, unwrap the wormery and you should be able to see how busy the worms have been. After the experiment, return the worms to the garden.

insect shelters

These shelters made from dried plant stems, moss and terracotta pots almost look like a natural feature of the garden. Hung in a sheltered position, the pots will provide refuge for insects, such as hibernating ladybirds and lacewings, and solitary bees, which may lay their eggs in the tubes, sealing them in with a mud bung. Each egg hatches into a grub that passes the winter as a cocoon and emerges as a bee in spring.

Materials

Terracotta flowerpots
Hollow dried plant stems (such as bamboo, fennel and giant thistles)
Moss
String

1 Cut the plant stems into lengths of roughly the same height as the pots and put a handful into each pot.

2 Tuck moss in and around the stems so they are held in position.

3 Tie a piece of string around the neck of each pot, leaving the ends long so they can be used to suspend them from a tree or bush.

things
to make
and do

Away from the constraints normally imposed inside the house, the garden is a perfect place for children to exercise their creativity and imagination, producing original, decorative and functional objects. Displaying children's whimsical artworks also personalizes the garden, imbuing it with a unique character and giving the children a stake in the fabric of the garden.

A wide range of craft materials will withstand the elements for at least a season or two, while others, such as mosaic, will last for years. Some paints are specifically designed for use outside, but many craft acrylics and emulsion paints will last for a couple of years, so it is worth experimenting.

The projects here do not have to be slavishly reproduced (although there is no reason why they shouldn't be), so there is plenty of opportunity for children to develop and use their own design ideas to fit the materials they have to hand.

colourful cane tops

Canes are very useful to stake plants, but their tops can be a hazard to gardeners and children as they work and play in the garden, potentially causing injuries to face and eyes. Decorative cane tops draw attention to the canes and give children a chance to show off their creative skills in adding their personal stamp to the garden.

Materials

Table tennis balls
Acrylic paint
Permanent waterproof markers
Lengths of 1-cm (⅜-in) diameter dowel

1 Paint the balls using different coloured paints. When dry, add your design with a permanent waterproof marker pen.

2 Ask an adult to help cut a cross in the base of the ball to create a hole larger enough to go over the cane.

3 Cut the dowel to the lengths required to support your plants. Push the decorated ball on to the top of the cane and repeat for the remaining balls until all the canes are covered.

4 If any of the cane tops need replacing, you can quickly make some more with different colours and designs.

weather monitoring station

This weather station is satisfying to construct, and will encourage children to consider the vicissitudes of the elements. A calibrated rain gauge allows them to monitor the exact amount of rainfall; a wind speed indicator shows just how fast the wind is blowing, while trailing streamers show its direction. Budding meteorologists will enjoy recording the rainfall and counting the wind-speed indicator, to build up their weather data.

Materials

3 bamboo barbecue skewers
3 table tennis balls (coloured if possible)
Strips of kite fabric or ribbon
170 cm (68 in) length of dowel
   (Note: the height of the station can be
   adapted to suit the height of the child.)
Insulation tape
Empty plastic bottle
Touch-and-close tape

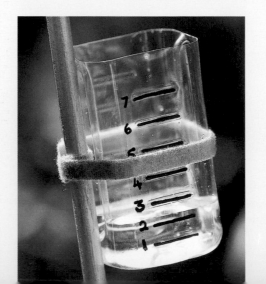

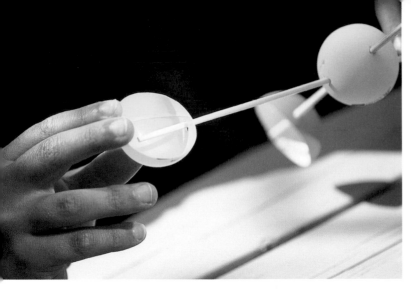

1 First, make the wind-speed indicator. Push two barbecue skewers through a table tennis ball so they form a cross. Holding this cross horizontally, pierce a hole in the base of the central ball (to attach it to the dowel at a later stage). Cut the other two table tennis balls in half. Under the rim of each half, pierce two holes opposite each other and mount them on to the ends of the skewers so the open sides are all facing in the same direction.

2 Attach the strips of kite fabric to one end of the remaining bamboo skewer. (You could use ribbon, but kite fabric is very light and will be caught by the gentlest of breezes.) Use insulation tape to bind the other end of the skewer to the top of the length of dowel.

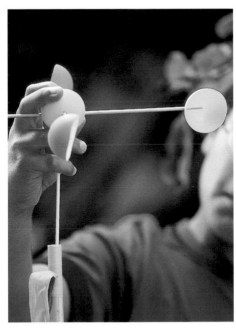

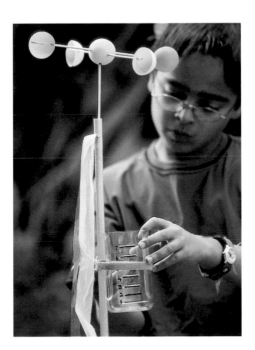

3 Now make the rain gauge. Cut the top from the plastic bottle and use a ruler and permanent marker pen to draw lines at regular intervals (either in metric or imperial measures) to indicate the rainfall.

4 Now assemble the station. Push the dowel into the ground and place the wind-speed indicator on the bamboo skewer at the top.

5 Attach the rain gauge to the length of dowel with the strip of touch-and-close tape, looping it tightly around the dowel and leaving a long loose end. This will hold the rain gauge in place but allow it to be removed and emptied easily.

green-haired scarecrow

A traditional part of the vegetable garden, this scarecrow's ability to keep away hungry birds may be in doubt, but his charm, wit, decorative value and the fun to be had building him make him a worthy addition to any garden. The opportunity to recycle favourite, outgrown clothes only adds to the appeal and comic personality. His mop of grass hair will need regular watering and can be kept neatly trimmed or left to grow long and wild.

Materials

280 cm (112 in) length of dowel
Twine
Old shirt and dungarees, or clothes of
  your choice
Large handkerchief
15 cm (6 in) terracotta pot
3 tacks
Small amount of loam-based compost
Small amount of grass seed

Why is grass green?

Plants transform sunlight into food. They do this by having hundreds of tiny structures called chloroplasts in their cells, which contain the light-collecting substance, chlorophyll. Chlorophyll is green and leaves are packed with it, which is why healthy grass is green.

1 Cut two lengths of dowel, one 180 cm (72 in) long and another 100 cm (39 in) long and use the twine to bind the two together to form a cross shape. The horizontal piece will be the scarecrow's arms and should be only about 20 cm (8 in) below the top of the vertical dowel.

2 Dress him in your chosen outfit (you may need to make a hole in the trousers for the dowel to go through). Push the scarecrow firmly into the ground, either in his permanent location or in a more convenient area to work on him (you can move him later).

3 Tightly knot the handkerchief around the 'neck' and place the terracotta pot on top of the vertical dowel to form the head. The knotted handkerchief should support the pot; if not, tap three tacks into the dowel under the pot to hold it steady.

4 Paint a simple face and, when the paint is dry, fill the pot with compost, firming it so the pot stands upright. Sprinkle grass seed on the compost and gently water it.

5 Move your scarecrow to his final position, if necessary, and push the dowel firmly into the ground to ensure it is stable. In a short time his green hair should begin to grow.

mosaic sundial

With this colourful sundial installed in the garden, learning to tell the time will be fun. Stand on the central stone of the sundial on a sunny day, arms stretched upwards, and the shadow cast will point to one of the mosaic numbers, indicating the time.

Here, randomly broken wall tiles have been used. For quicker results, the numbers could be painted on to the paving stones using masonry paint.

Materials
9 paving stones 20 x 20 cm (8 x 8 in)
30–40 broken ceramic tiles
Cement-based tile adhesive
Cement-based tile grout

⚠️ *Note: Safety goggles should be worn when smashing tiles.*

1 Using a pencil, draw the numbers from 9 to 12 and 1 to 4, one on each paving slab. This means your sundial will work from 9 a.m. to 4 p.m. On the final slab, draw your design for the central stone (we used a pair of feet, see page 107). To break the tiles, place them on a board, cover with a cloth and gently tap them with a hammer.

2 Mix up the tile adhesive according to the manufacturer's instructions and, using a spatula, spread a thin layer of adhesive following the shape of the first number. Push pieces of tile into the adhesive, leaving thin gaps of about 5 mm (¼ in) between pieces. Once the number is complete, use the same method to complete the background. Make mosaics of the other seven numbers in the same way.

3 When the adhesive has dried, mix up enough grout to complete one paving stone. Spread the grout on to the surface of the mosaic with a sponge, pushing it between the pieces of tile.

4 Wipe the excess grout from the surface of the tiles, and, when the grout has dried slightly, polish the surface with a clean cloth.

5 Choose a sunny site and place the central stone on the ground, with the mosaic feet pointing away from the sun at midday. Then, every hour from 9 a.m. to 4 p.m., stand on the stone with arms stretched upwards and place the corresponding mosaic number at the tip of the shadow.

6 Once the positions have been marked, the number stones can be set in place by cutting out a section of turf and bedding the stones on sharp sand flush with the lawn.

7 You will need a team of friends to help you position the numbered tiles, and, once they are in place you can each take a turn at testing the sundial.

ABOVE *The sundial provides a great tool for discussing how the sun appears to move across the sky and how the earth rotates.*

LEFT *Drawing around your feet makes a fitting design and personalizes the central mosaic, although any design could be chosen if you wish.*

flashing bird scarer

Having spent hours tending your fruit and vegetable garden, watching the progress of each crop and eagerly anticipating the harvest, it is very frustrating to find that you have been beaten to it by the birds! However welcome they may be in some parts of the garden, birds are to be discouraged from others, and these animated, sparkling mobiles should keep them off the vegetable patch.

Materials

Compact discs
Enamel craft paint in two colours
PVA glue or silicone sealant
1m (3 ft) of 5-mm (¼-in) diameter dowel
Elastic thread
Wooden skewer

1 Using enamel paint, decorate the most reflective surface of the compact discs. Don't cover the whole surface, so the shiny CD coating still shows through. Leave them to dry.

2 Attach the unpainted side of one of the compact discs to the end of the skewer using PVA glue or silicone sealant.

3 Attach another compact disc to the other side of the skewer, so the skewer is sandwiched between the two decorated discs. Leave them to dry. Now add the other pair of discs further down the skewer by the same method, but at right angles to the first pair.

4 Tie a length of elastic thread to the end of the skewer and then attach this to the end of the dowel, so that the mobile is suspended on about 10–15 cm (4–6 in) of elastic.

5 Finally, push the bird scarer into the soil among the plants you want to protect. Set it at an angle so the discs can spin freely.

fragrant tree seat

This colourful take on a tree seat provides the perfect spot for children to perch. Its fragrant 'cushion' will produce an irresistible burst of spicy scent every time it is used.

A triumph of recycling, the tyres can be painted and decorated with any colourful design to suit their surroundings. Both the fig tree and seat plants will appreciate a warm, sheltered spot and should grow well for several years in the confines of the tyre container.

Materials

2 tyres
Pink multi-purpose spray paint
Green and blue acrylic paint
Gravel
Loam-based compost
Fig tree
5 creeping thyme or chamomile plants

1 First, decorate the tyres. Clean them thoroughly and paint the outsides and walls with spray paint. Leave them to dry before adding the decoration. Here, simple grass and flowers have been added using single stokes of the brush and spots of paint.

2 Place the tyres in their final position, one on top of the other. (Once constructed, the seat is very difficult to move.) Put a layer of gravel in the bottom and fill the tyres three-quarters full of compost.

3 Plant the fig tree at the centre of the tyres, firming more compost around it so that the compost level is flush with the wall of the tyre. Add the thyme or chamomile plants around the fig tree and water them in.

Keeping your seat in trim

LEFT *The handsome leaves of the fig will eventually cast a dappled shade over the tree seat.* ABOVE *Trimming the thyme, once it is established, will help to keep it compact and encourage it to form a dense mat of fragrant foliage that will provide a green and perfumed cushion for any visitor.*

willow den

Green, lush and evocative of woodland or jungle hideaways, a leafy den appeals to children of all ages as a place to play with friends or as a private space to spend time alone or with a good book. The leafy dome sits easily in the garden and is almost invisible when built among trees or shrubs – a small den can even be slipped into the back of a border. This den is 3 m (10 ft) in diameter, but a den can be made to fit into any available space.

Materials

Weed-suppressing membrane
6 thick withies
50 thinner withies
Raffia
Play bark

Keeping the shape
Planted in the dormant period, the willow rods – called withies – used to construct the den will root and grow easily as spring arrives. New shoots can be woven back into the structure, increasing the feeling of privacy inside the dome. Keeping the shape tidy is easy: in winter, just remove any unwanted growth; you could even cut it back to the original framework.

1 Use a peg and string to mark out a circle with a 1.5 m (5 ft) radius (see page 19). Remove the turf within the circle and dig garden compost into the outer 30 cm (1 ft) of the circle.

2 Lay weed-suppressing membrane over the entire circle. Pin the membrane down securely at the edges and allow an overlap of about 20 cm (8 in) where the strips meet. Trim the edges to follow the shape of the circle.

3 Now make the doorway. Cut two small holes in the membrane about 50 cm (20 in) apart, and push two of the thinner withies through the holes into the ground to a depth of about 20 cm (8 in). Bend each one towards the other and twist them together to form an arch. Tie the ends securely with raffia.

4 Next, take the six thicker withies and space them equally around the remaining circumference of the circle. Push them in as before, and arch them to the centre, tying them securely so that they form a dome shape.

5 Start filling in between the main structural withies with the thinner ones. Work around the structure, pushing more withies into the ground at an angle so they point in the direction you are working. Space them regularly. Now work back the other way, angling the withies so they criss-cross each other.

6 With all the withies firmly pushed into the ground, work around the structure, weaving them in and out of each other up the length of each withie, gently forming a domed shape.

7 As you progress, tie the woven withies on to the vertical structural withies to create the dome. Use ties at any other point to hold the withies in position, especially at the top of the dome.

8 Finally, weave a number of withies horizontally through the structure to form a band two or three withies wide about three-quarters of the way up. Spread a layer of play bark in the den, and it's ready for occupation.

ABOVE *Simple logs are the perfect way to furnish the leafy den, so long as all sharp edges are removed. Provide a few basics and children will soon organize their own den how they want it.*

RIGHT *The den makes a great place to play even before it has a full covering of leaves . Once established, the den requires little maintenance beyond its annual trim, but it may require watering.*

pot decorations

Easy to make, colourful pot decorations are great for cheering up container plants when they don't look their best, adding a touch of humour or just giving a planted pot a touch of character. They are also a fun way for children to exercise their creativity and exhibit the results in the garden. Give the children a selection of decorative materials and they will come up with a plethora of designs, or inspire them with some of the examples shown here.

Materials

Paper
3 sheets of craft foam in different
*   colours (including yellow)*
Bamboo skewers
PVA glue

> ⚠️ **Note:** *When using skewers as the basis for pot decorations, be careful not to leave an exposed point at the top.*

1 Draw a flower shape on a sheet of paper, or trace a motif, and cut out with scissors. Use this template to cut out a flower from the foam and add a yellow circle in the centre with PVA glue.

2 Plant out some hyacinth bulbs in terracotta pots, with the top of the bulbs just above the compost. Keep moist and warm and the flowers will soon blossom.

3 Attach the flower to a wooden skewer with PVA glue and stick it into the compost to add another bloom to the pots.

LEFT *This dragonfly cut from craft foam looks at home among grasses and would be a stunning addition to a container pond, which might even attract real dragonflies. Simple shapes are very effective. Children can either draw around a template or work freehand using a felt-tip pen, and any errors can always be hidden on the reverse of the finished decoration.*

BELOW *Iridescent glass stars sparkle among the foliage of herbs. Quick and easy to make, the stars are mounted on a bamboo skewer using silicon sealant or PVA glue, producing these simple but effective decorations.*

ABOVE *Even the show-stopping, dazzling flowers of the gerbera can be given a lift with a pot decoration. Colourful plastic beads threaded on to bamboo barbecue skewers and pushed into the compost of the pot set off the delicious orange of the gerbera. Inexpensive beads are well suited to this task, as long as the holes are large enough to fit over the skewer.*

RIGHT *In this variation, the decoration is formed by plastic drinking straws, cut into lengths, pierced at their centre and threaded on to the skewer. They form a swirl of colour that can be either suspended from a cane or hung from above.*

customized garden boots

Personalizing your boots with designs inspired by plants and wildlife is a great way to ensure you stand out in the crowd. Even the youngest children can make their mark on their own boots, perhaps using stamps or sponges rather than painting freehand. If things go wrong, the paints can be wiped from the rubber while still wet. Once dry, the decorations should last for as long as the boots last the children.

Materials

Rubber boots
Very fine sandpaper
Enamel or acrylic paints

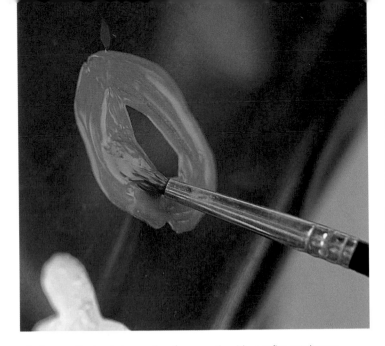

1 Prepare the boots by sanding them gently with very fine sandpaper. Mark on your design with water-based felt-tip pens. Paint in the design.

2 Clean your brush before applying different colours and leave the painting to dry overnight. You can add details once the paint is dry.

Fun designs

Taking inspiration from the garden seems most appropriate, and these daisies are a simple design to copy. Simple, bold shapes are the easiest to achieve, as the paint sits on the surface of the rubber for some time before it dries. A watery theme is a good choice for wet, weather wear.

lots of labels

Labelling each plant and seedling with its name and perhaps the date of planting is a useful habit to learn, but labels don't have to be utilitarian or dull. There are plenty of everyday materials children can use to create their own fun and imaginative labels that will add character and wit to the garden. Making them becomes a pleasurable activity in itself. Labels for trays of seedlings are not required for long, but it is worth investing time in making something that will last for plants that are a permanent part of the garden.

RIGHT A simple shell tucked into the side of this decorated trough of sempervivums imparts a seaside feel. Using a permanent marker ensures the lettering won't fade.

ABOVE *Nestled among the thyme, a smooth, blue-grey pebble has been painted with acrylic paint. The colour has been chosen carefully to look good against the thyme.*

RIGHT *A recycled wooden gift tag has been spruced up with a coat of paint and provides a smart label for this little lollipop lavender.*

FAR RIGHT *A wooden clothes peg has the advantage of being easy to attach to the edge of pots and seed trays. Permanent marker pens will provide long-lasting labels.*

ABOVE *Giving the pot a coat of blackboard paint (which comes in several colours other than black) solves the label problem completely – as long as the weather stays dry, that is, or the pots are kept in a greenhouse. The name of the plant can be written straight on to the pot and wiped off easily when it becomes home to a new plant.*

LEFT *Shapes cut from craft foam, and mounted on a bamboo skewer or an ice-lolly stick make striking labels that really add to a pot's appeal. The vibrant lime green sets off the yellow narcissi beautifully.*

RIGHT *An old favourite, ice-lolly sticks can be smartened up with a coat of paint to make practical and stylish labels.*

summer flower and leaf party

With just a few simple activities and a feast for hungry revellers, this garden party will entertain a group of children all afternoon. Involving children as much with the planning and preparation as with the party itself is immensely enjoyable and gives them a fantastic sense of achievement. As the garden is the central theme of the party as well as the venue, the activities encourage children to look at the garden in a new way.

Garden crowns

Creating a crown to wear during the party is an excellent way to start the occasion, and will keep early arrivals occupied while you wait for all the guests to assemble. Suggest the children take their inspiration from the garden: this will help focus their activity.

All you need to have ready are:
- strips of thin card (have some spares to hand, so that any spoilt attempts can be started afresh)
- plenty of felt-tip pens
- gift ribbon
- a few fresh flowers

When the children have finished their decoration, staple the strip into a crown shape to fit their head and add ribbons at the back and flowers at the side for those who want them.

Butterfly and blossom tree

Festooned with vibrant blossoms and intricate butterflies, this tree looks like something from Wonderland! Working together to make a host of fanciful paper butterflies and flowers to decorate a tree or bush is an absorbing, exciting finale to the party. The tree is transformed into something thrilling and very special and is a satisfying reward for all the children's hard work.

All you will need to supply is:
- coloured paper
- scissors (depending upon the ages of the children, you can either prepare plenty of flower and butterfly shapes ready cut out, or provide the paper and round-ended scissors and let them draw and cut out their own)
- felt-tip pens
- hole punch
- fine thread to attach them to the tree

Leaf hunt

Even small gardens are likely to contain an amazingly diverse collection of differently shaped and coloured leaves. Setting children the task of collecting as many different leaves as they can and mounting them on a large card leaf will keep them busy for some time. The challenge of finding as many examples as possible will inspire children in their quest and prompt them, possibly for the first time, to look closely at leaf shapes and colours.

Check the garden beforehand for plants that the children should not pick from. There may be hazardous plants, such as euphorbias, which exude an irritant sap when leaves are removed, or toxic plants (see page 138), or simply very young specimens that might not survive young fingers tugging at them enthusiastically. Remove them or fence them off.

Before the children arrive, cut large leaf shapes from thin card, one for each child, and supply glue or adhesive tape with which to attach their leaves. After the leaf hunt, encourage the children to wash their hands.

Party feast

No party is complete without a feast. After running around, children will be hungry and thirsty, so provide plenty of appealing party food.

Place names decorated with pressed flowers from the garden are in keeping with the party's theme. These are something your own child or children can work on days before the party. Pick perfect blooms from the garden, sandwich them between sheets of blotting paper and press them between heavy books or in a flower press.

Cut rectangles of card, glue a pressed flower to the end of each and write on a guest's name.

Bring the garden into the party food too: decorate cakes and puddings with crystallized flowers or petals (see page 67), add freshly picked herbs and edible flowers wherever you can (see page 64), make drinks pretty with petals and if the timing is right there may even be fruit or vegetables to pick straight from the garden (see pages 52–71).

psychedelic mobile

Hanging from a tree or pergola, this mobile can be relied upon to decorate the garden with a splash of vibrant colour all year round. It is made from easy-to-use craft foam and the hoops and discs are so light that they will rotate in the slightest breath of wind. You can make the mobile as long or as short as you wish, or perhaps hang a group of them together for more impact.

Materials

4 sheets of craft foam in 4 different
colours
Nylon thread
Drinking straw
PVA glue

Tip

The leftover foam is useful for other
projects, such as pot decorations
(see page 116).

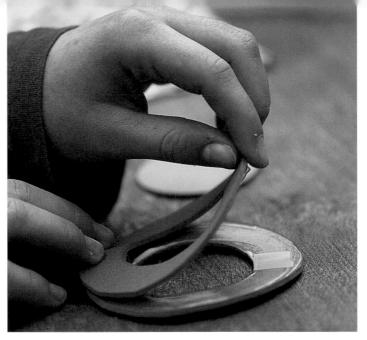

1 Using a felt-tip pen, draw two concentric circles of about 15 cm (6 in) and 12 cm (5 in) diameter on the craft foam. (Young children will find it easiest to draw around cups or perhaps card templates.) Cut them out to make a hoop. Make two hoops of each colour.

2 Spread one side of a hoop with PVA glue. Cut two short lengths of drinking straw not more than 2.5 cm (1 in) long and place them opposite each other on the hoop and place another hoop on top, pressing them together firmly. Do the same with the other hoops, giving you four double-thickness hoops.

3 Cut ten foam discs the same size as the central hole in the hoops. (Older children may be able to cut the hoops so the centres remain intact and use these instead.) Take a length of nylon thread and glue two of the discs together, sandwiching one end of the thread.

4 Pass the nylon thread through the two pieces of straw of one of the hoops. Then add another pair of discs. Keep adding discs and hoops alternately until the mobile is complete. When all the glue is thoroughly dry, tie the mobile in position.

pot pourri

Children are instinctively drawn by scents in the garden, smelling flowers and crushing leaves and stalks. Making pot pourri takes this a stage further, encouraging them to seek out flowers and foliage to preserve. You can use a few drops of essential oil to strengthen the fragrance, or add spices such as cloves, cinnamon sticks and nutmeg. Dried autumn berries, seed heads and citrus peel all make colourful additions.

Materials

Flowers and foliage for drying
Essential oils
Fixative (see below)

Staying power
To make the fragrance last you will need to include a fixative, which holds the scent better than the dried flowers alone. Cloves, chamomile flowers, nutmeg or cinnamon sticks are the most readily available fixatives.

1 Gather a selection of flowers and foliage from the garden. Pick each of them with a good length of stem, and choose only flowers that are dry and in good condition.

2 Remove all the leaves from the flower stems and tie them into small bunches, so the blooms are not too crowded.

3 Hang the bunches of flowers in a warm, airy place away from strong sunlight. Even at this stage the bunches of drying flowers make a pretty decoration. How long they take to dry will depend on the size of flower and where they are dried.

4 Once the flowers are completely dry, mix a few drops of essential oil with your fixative in a large bowl. Then add the flower heads and mix them gently. Put the mix in an airtight container or plastic bag and keep it in a dark place for about a month. Your pot pourri is then ready.

christmas garland

A string of seed heads and fir cones sparkling with silvery frost is the perfect adornment for bare trees and shrubs at this time of year. The garlands are straightforward and quick to make. Gathering the materials to form the garland encourages children into the garden to hunt for skeletal seed heads and other treasures to decorate, prompting them to look closely at what is happening in the garden and its stark beauty at this time of year.

Materials

Dried seed heads
Fir cones
Wire
Silver spray paint

1 Collect seed heads and cones from the garden. If you don't have anything suitable in your garden, you could gather them from hedgerows and roadsides or on a woodland walk.

2 Trim the stalks of the seed heads to about 10 cm (4 in) long and spray them and the fir cones silver. Leave them to dry.

3 Take a length of wire and twist it to form loops at irregularly spaced intervals along its length. Push the stems of the seed heads through the loops. Now intersperse these with the fir cones, attaching them by twisting the wire through the cone.

4 The garland is then ready to adorn any tree or bush in the garden that needs lifting with a touch of Christmas sparkle.

safety

Tireless explorers, children are always testing and experimenting with everything around them, and minor mishaps and injuries inevitably arise from this relentless pursuit of experience. What is important is that gardens where children play should be as safe as possible, so parents can confidently allow them the freedom to play unrestricted. One of the difficulties is that potential hazards change with the age of the child and from child to child.

Essentially, providing a safe space to play and explore is common sense: not leaving sharp or heavy tools unattended, even while you answer the phone; protecting expanses of standing water and keeping all garden chemicals and products securely locked away. Regular maintenance and checks on play equipment will ensure they are kept in good condition.

Less obvious is the threat from plants. In this book, children are encouraged to become passionate about plants – to grow fruit and vegetables, as well as flowers to eat, and to enjoy the fragrance of flowers and foliage. It is essential that they learn to discriminate and understand that some plants are harmful and they can eat or even pick only those that an adult has told them is safe. Many of the most common garden plants are toxic, while others, such as euphorbias, exude an irritant sap that will produce a severe allergic reaction. Plants with sharp spines or pointed leaves present the danger of physical injury. Excluding the most hazardous of plants from the garden while children are young is the safest option. Exhaustive lists of hazardous plants are readily available; unfortunately space does not allow one to be reproduced here.

The creative projects in this book encourage children to experiment with a vast array of materials. Again safety is a matter of common sense and the level of supervision will depend upon the age and capabilities of the child. Where possible, however, buy non-toxic paints and choose craft tools, such as scissors, designed especially for children.

Index

Acknowledgements

Author acknowledgements

My thanks: To Harriet, Nancy, Joshua, Molly, Florence, Jemima, Robbie, Jessica, Nicholas, Connie, Ollie, Jessie, Roma, William and Carragh who enliven the pages of this book with their fantastic smiles.

To Clive Nichols for his splendid photography and boundless enthusiasm.

To my parents, Ruth and Geoffrey Smee, for, once again, helping out in a myriad of ways.

To Sarah Ford, Jessica Cowie and everyone at Hamlyn who worked on the project.

To Richard Kerwood of Windrush Willow (www.windrushwillow.com), for supplying fantastic withies at short notice.

To Bob Hussain of Gardenscape Supplies, Playhatch for all his help.

And finally, to my children, Harriet, Nancy and Joshua for their inspiration and invaluable insight and criticism.

Executive Editor Sarah Ford
Project Editor Jessica Cowie
Executive Art Editor Joanna MacGregor
Designer Peter Gerrish
Production Manager Ian Paton
All projects created and styled by Clare Matthews